Unlocking Financial Potential

Mastering Business Credit for Growth and Prosperity

By

Damian Clarke

Table of Contents

Securing Financial Prosperity by Mastering Business Credit

Introduction

Access to financial resources is the lifeblood of every successful firm, despite the constantly changing world of entrepreneurship and commerce. Whether you're a seasoned business person looking to build your company or an ambitious startup founder with a big idea, your ability to use the power of business credit may be the key to achieving unheard-of growth and wealth.

The detailed manual "Unlocking Financial Potential: Mastering Business Credit for Growth and Prosperity" will help you understand the complex world of company finance. We shall set out on a trip inside these pages to not only comprehend the subtleties of company credit but also to strategically and ethically use it to power your objectives.

Business credit is important across all sectors and sizes of operations. It's the instrument that may enable you to take advantage of development prospects that were previously out of your grasp, acquire advantageous loans, build relationships with suppliers, etc. But to master this instrument, you must have knowledge, discipline, and a well-thought-out plan.

This book is intended to provide you with the information, tactics, and insights required to successfully negotiate the complex world of business finance. The ideas presented here are relevant to your journey regardless of whether you're just getting started or have been in the company for a while, whether you're beginning from scratch or want to reenergize your financial strategy.

You'll get a little bit closer to your financial goals with each chapter. This book is your road map to success, from comprehending the principles of company credit to creating effective credit applications, properly managing credit, and eventually reaching financial prosperity.

You'll learn about the theoretical foundations of business credit in the chapters that follow, as well as case studies from actual firms that demonstrate how it can alter companies of all sizes and sectors. You'll have access to useful tools and information along the road to guide your choices and set you on the path to financial wealth.

Therefore, let's start this adventure together and unleash the limitless financial potential that lies ahead, whether your objective is to get that crucial company loan, increase operations, or just solidify your financial base. Here you will find information on "Unlocking Financial Potential: Mastering Business Credit for Growth and Prosperity."

Chapter 1

The Influence of Business Credit

When someone begins a firm, they often may not have access to huge quantities of money or are motivated to seek seed financing, like many small-business owners around the nation. So, it stands to reason that utilizing funds and asking for personal loans or credit cards is the most typical method a new business owner launches their venture.

My first business ventures followed a similar course, but I soon saw that I required additional funding to scale up my infrastructure and marketing efforts to stand out from the crowd.

What I discovered very early on was that if you over-leverage your credit profile by taking out many loans or maxing out your credit cards to finance your company, your personal life may be damaged very rapidly due to the bad influence on your credit score.

What is Business Credit

Business credit is a distinct credit profile that you build in the name of your company from your credit profile. You may lessen the financial load on your personal finances and credit profile by successfully establishing a company credit profile.

By doing this, you open yourself up to more personal possibilities and keep the greatest interest rates on personal loans, insurance premiums, and other credit-related transactions.

How therefore can you begin establishing a sound company credit profile? There are a few requirements to meet before you can start acquiring financing and credit under your company name.

The compass that directs your trip while pursuing any ambitious endeavor is clear, relevant objectives. Defining your financial goals is a vital first step in understanding company credit for development and profitability. A company without clearly defined financial objectives may struggle to chart its route, just as a ship without a direction may drift aimlessly.

- **Defining Your Vision**

Every successful company endeavor has a strong and appealing vision at its core. Your vision acts as a compass, pointing you in the direction of the future you want. It's more than simply a declaration of your goals; it's a clear mental image of the difference you want to have in your field, your neighborhood, and the whole globe. Determining your vision is the crucial first step toward financial success in the area of managing company credit for development and wealth.

- **The Strength of Vision**

A clear vision serves as a source of inspiration and drive. It gives your company a new life by giving it a purpose and a direction. A vision may give your path direction and provide you the concentration you need to overcome obstacles and take advantage of the possibilities that lie ahead.

Important Components of Your Vision

- Clarity: You and your team should both be able to clearly understand your vision. There should be no space for interpretation.
- Although short-term objectives are important, your vision is a long-term

ideal. It needs to include your vision for your company in five, 10, or even twenty years.

- Alignment: Your vision needs to be in line with your beliefs, interests, and the primary goal of your company. It ought to be consistent with your values and function as motivation for your everyday activities.
- Innovation: A compelling vision often questions the existing quo and fosters creativity. It motivates you to use your imagination and look for potential development opportunities.
- Inspiration: Your vision needs to motivate not just you but also your coworkers, business associates, and clients. People need to desire to support and participate in it.

How to Defining Your Vision in Steps

- Consider Your Purpose: Start by considering the main reason why you are in business. Why is it there? What issues does it address? How does it make its stakeholders' lives better?

- Think about how your company might seem in the ideal future if it realized all of its potential. Consider the effect it would have on your market, your clients, and the whole planet.
- Write it down and describe your vision. Create a vision statement that expresses the core of your goals. Be succinct, effective, and unforgettable.
- Share and refine your vision with important constituencies, including your staff and advisers. Your vision may be strengthened and improved with their input.
- Review and revisit: As your company develops and evolves, your vision could shift. To make sure it continues to be in line with your aims and values, review and revisit it often.

Your vision is a dynamic force that should direct the development of your company; it is not static. You'll learn as we go along in this book how controlling business credit can be a crucial instrument in realizing your vision. You may be able to get the capital you need to support your expansion and realize your dreams by using business financing. So, when you go out on your path to manage company credit for development and wealth, let your vision serve as your North Star.

Long-Term vs. Short-Term Goals

Identifying short-term and long-term objectives is essential if you're serious about managing company credit and reaching financial success. These two types of objectives play separate but complementary roles in determining the course of your company. Sustainable development and success depend on knowing when and how to use each kind.

Short-Term Objectives: Getting Around the Present

The stepping stones that lead your company through the near future are short-term objectives. Usually, they last for a few days, weeks, or months. These objectives fulfill a number of crucial purposes:

- Immediate Focus: Short-term objectives support ongoing corporate operations and take immediate action on critical issues. They give us a feeling of direction and urgency.
- Short-term objectives enable swift adaptability to shifting conditions in a dynamic corporate environment. They aid in your ability to react to new possibilities and difficulties.
- Momentum: Reaching short-term objectives may boost your team's morale and momentum. Small successes might pave the way for bigger ones.

In the context of corporate financing, some examples of short-term objectives may be:

- ☐ Reducing unpaid supplier debt during the next three months.
- ☐ Raising your company's credit score by 10 points over the next two billing cycles.
- ☐ Satisfying a forthcoming project's urgent working capital requirements.

Long-Term Objectives: Planning for the Future

On the other hand, long-term objectives are lofty dreams that extend into the future. They include the main goals of your company and may include a period expressed in years or even decades. Long-term objectives provide strategic meaning and direction:

- Long-term objectives guarantee that your company maintains alignment with its fundamental purpose and values. They act as a north star, directing significant choices and financial commitments.
- Long-term objectives encourage sustainability by promoting a forward-thinking attitude. They assist you in creating a company that can survive changes in the market and economic cycles.
- Growth and prosperity: attaining these objectives is essential for attaining both significant growth and material affluence. They stand for achievements that, if

achieved, may change the size and influence of your company.

Examples of long-term objectives about company credit may be:

- ☐ Developing into a favored borrower with access to bigger loan lines over the next five years.
- ☐ Expansion of your company into new markets or areas over the following ten years, made possible by solid credit ties.
- ☐ Building credit so that your company may get loans at cheap interest rates for long-term expansion.

The Balance between Short-Term and Long-Term Objectives

While they may seem to conflict with one another, short- and long-term objectives are complimentary. The tactical flexibility required to get closer to your long-term vision is provided by short-term objectives. They make sure you remain on track while adjusting to current difficulties.

SMART Goals are Specific, Measurable, Attainable, Relevant, and Time Bound.

Any successful endeavor must start with setting objectives, but not all goals are made equal. Make sure your objectives are SMART: specific, measurable, achievable, relevant, and time-bound to guarantee they are useful and actionable.

- **Specific**

A particular aim is specified with clarity, precision, and detail. There is no place for doubt or misunderstanding in it. Think about the "W" questions while establishing particular objectives:

- ☐ What do you want to achieve?
- ☐ Why is this objective crucial?
- ☐ Who is concerned?
- ☐ Where is it going to happen?
- ☐ Which limitations or specifications apply?

A detailed, SMART goal might be, "Increase our business credit score by 20 points within the next six months to qualify for a lower-interest loan." As an example, a general aim may be, to "Improve business credit."

- **Measurable**

Measurable objectives are measurable and provide a way to monitor your development. They respond to inquiries like:

- ☐ How much development is necessary?
- ☐ How many or how frequently?
- ☐ How will you know when the objective has been met?

Progress must be measured to maintain motivation and make required corrections. A quantifiable objective for corporate credit may be to "reduce outstanding debts by 15% within the next quarter."

- **Achievable**

Realistic and reachable objectives are doable. It takes into account the tools, abilities, and limitations you have at your disposal. Although setting lofty objectives is necessary, they should also be attainable. Think about it:

- ☐ Is this objective feasible in light of your existing situation?

☐ Do you possess the tools required to do it?
☐ Is it possible to do it before the deadline?

A goal like "Increase annual revenue by 500% within a month" could not be feasible for most firms.

Relevant

A goal is relevant if it is consistent with your overarching goals and purpose. It needs to be significant and aid in the expansion and success of your company. Consider:

☐ Is this objective relevant to your long-term goals?
☐ Will it assist you in getting closer to your long-term goals?
☐ Is it reasonable in light of your existing priorities?

Building solid credit connections with key suppliers to guarantee a consistent supply of inventory for our increasing product range would be a pertinent aim in the area of company credit.

- **Time-Bound**

A time-bound objective has a set completion date or period. As a result, there is a feeling of responsibility and urgency. Consider the following issues:

- ☐ When will you begin working on this objective?
- ☐ When do you anticipate achieving it?
- ☐ What are the along-the-road intermediate checkpoints?

Setting a deadline helps you stay focused and prevents objectives from becoming open-ended. A time-bound objective would be, "Secure a business line of credit with a $50,000 limit by the end of the next quarter."

Aligning Business and Financial Objectives

Recognizing that your financial goals should effortlessly connect with your larger company objectives is essential if you want to achieve financial wealth and commercial success. Your financial objectives will become a potent force propelling the expansion, sustainability, and general success of your business if these two factors are well aligned.

The Relationship Is Symbiotic

Financial and business objectives are mutually beneficial. Your financial objectives provide the means to finance and support those desires, while your company goals reflect your vision, purpose, and growth strategy. Let's look at some successful ways to promote this alignment:

- Your company objectives should come first since they should be the cornerstone around which your financial goals are constructed. Start by outlining the long- and short-term goals for your company. Think about issues like:
- What is your main goal?
- What markets or clientele do you want to serve?
- What goods or services do you intend to provide?
- What development trajectory do you want to achieve?

- Once your company's objectives have been established, determine the financial requirements needed to carry them out. Dependencies on money include things like:

1. Capital requirements: How much money is required to sustain operations and growth?
2. Cash flow management: How will you make sure that there is a steady flow of cash to pay bills and make investments in expansion?
3. What sorts of loans or funding are required to carry out your company plans?

- Establish particular financial goals that are in line with your company's objectives after having a thorough awareness of the financial realities of your company. These objectives have to be SMART, which stands for Specific, Measurable, Achievable, Relevant, and Time-Bound.
- Maintain a close eye on your progress toward your financial and professional objectives. To keep your financial objectives in line with your growing company plan, make any necessary adjustments.

Illustrations of Alignment

Take into account the following instances to demonstrate how business and financial objectives are compatible:

- Business Objective: Increase market share by introducing goods in new geographies.
1. Financial Goal: Obtain a company line of credit to support the market growth to produce a 20% increase in revenue within the following year.
- Improve customer service and product quality to increase consumer happiness and loyalty.
1. Financial Goal: Establish a budget for training and technology improvements to improve customer support skills, with a target of a 15% rise in repeat business and customer retention over the following two years.
- Establish your company as a pioneer in sustainable business practices in your sector.
1. Financial Goal: Over five years, enhance profitability by 10% by investing in

environmentally friendly manufacturing methods and materials to cut expenses of operations and draw in eco-aware clients.

The Function of Business Credit in Achieving Your Objectives

You may reach your financial and professional objectives by using the dynamic and powerful weapon of business finance. Strategically using corporate finance may help your company achieve new levels of expansion, sustainability, and profitability. This section will examine the many ways that company credit might help you achieve your goals.

- Capital Access

Having the capacity to obtain funds when you need them is one of the most immediate and palpable advantages of managing company credit. Business credit provides a variety of financial options to fulfill your capital requirements, whether you're trying to finance an expansion, buy new equipment, or just manage cash flow during slower times.

- Business Loans: Term loans, working capital loans, and equipment financing may provide you with the money you need for a variety of things, from starting a marketing campaign to recruiting new employees.

1. Business Lines of Credit: These adaptable credit lines provide you the flexibility to withdraw money as required, acting as a backup plan for unforeseen costs or possibilities.
2. Business credit cards provide a practical means to pay for daily costs while also accruing incentives or cashback.
- Developing a Credit History

Establishing and maintaining good business credit is similar to establishing a solid financial standing for your firm. A good credit history affects the terms and interest rates you are offered as well as your ability to get loans. Having a good credit history can:

1. Reduce Borrowing Costs: Having good credit may result in loans and credit lines with reduced interest rates over time, saving your company money.
2. Attract Partners and Suppliers: A strong credit history may help you win the confidence of investors, partners, and

suppliers, leading to fruitful partnerships and business prospects.

- Risk Mitigation

Additionally, business credit is a risk-management instrument. It enables you to separate your personal and corporate funds, safeguarding your assets from obligations incurred by your firm. For the sake of preserving your financial stability, this separation may be essential.

- Encouraging Growth

Business financing often serves as a link between current circumstances and desired outcomes for companies with ambitious development goals. You can

1. Expand Operations: Obtain funding to establish more sites, hire more employees, or spend money on marketing initiatives to reach a wider audience.

2. Invest in Innovation: To remain inventive and competitive, fund R&D, technological updates, and product diversity.
3. Seize possibilities: Be prepared to seize possibilities when they present themselves, such as buying out a rival, getting a deal on inventory, or increasing production.

- Controlling cash flow

Effective cash flow management is essential for your company's ongoing stability and expansion. As a safety net, business credit may help you overcome brief cash flow shortfalls, pay suppliers on time, and maintain the efficiency of your operations.

- Scaling Carefully

Controlling your finances becomes more important as your firm grows. Business credit gives you the resources you need to grow responsibly, helping you to handle growing financial complexity while sticking to your objectives and plans.

Chapter 2

Establishing a Solid Credit Foundation

By building a solid credit foundation, you may start your road to mastering business credit. A solid credit foundation offers the stability and power your company needs to scale new heights, much as a solid and sturdy foundation supports a tall building. This chapter will examine the fundamental procedures and ideas involved in laying this important foundation.

Knowledge of Business Credit

What is business credit?

Different from your credit profile, corporate credit is a credit history established in your company's name. You may lessen the financial burden on your credit profile and your finances if you can successfully build a company credit profile.

By doing this, you open yourself up to more personal possibilities and keep the greatest interest rates on personal loans, insurance premiums, and other credit-related transactions.

How therefore can you begin establishing a sound company credit profile? To start being accepted for credit and capital purely in your company's name, there are a few things to take. However, you must first provide the groundwork for doing so.

Developing a Business Credit Profile

When seeking to build a company credit profile, the first thing to consider is whether or not you are set up as a business. It's critical to recognize that banks and other lenders must examine your firm independently of you. I'm advising you to establish a distinct credit profile, thus your company must be properly set up as a separate legal organization.

Establishing a company with your secretary of state and obtaining an employment identification number are both important steps, but it's also crucial that all the information be accurate. If not, building credibility for your company would be difficult.

You should also set up a business location, company phone number, and business bank account as additional crucial stages in laying the right foundation. Your personal phone number, address, and bank account must all be kept separate from all of these.

No matter how basic, make sure you have a website. Following your domain purchase, a lot of internet domain providers provide a free website builder that you may put up immediately. Obtaining an email address that is an extension of your website is a good idea after buying the domain and setting up your website. Therefore, if your website's domain name is "www.joesbbq.com," you should set up an email address that begins with "Joe@joesbbq.com."

Keeping Your Personal Credit History Clear

How Do Credit Reports Work?

Your credit history is a record of the obligations you have repaid and the maturity with which you have done so. It is included in your credit report, which also includes information on the number and kinds of credit accounts you have, as well as their ages, balances outstanding, how much of your available credit has been utilized, whether you pay your bills on time, and the number of recent credit inquiries. Your credit report also details any bankruptcies, liens, collections, or judgments that you may have.

Main Points

- Your credit history is a record of your capacity to repay debts and your track record of doing so responsibly.
- The number and kinds of credit accounts you have are included on your credit report. In addition, credit histories include information on how long each account has been active, how much is owed, how much of the available credit has been utilized, whether invoices were paid on time and the frequency of recent credit queries.
- A solid credit history has advantages, such as increasing your likelihood of being accepted for loans with reduced interest rates.
- Your credit history is the foundation of your credit score.

Exactly Why Credit History Is Crucial

Your credit history is used by prospective creditors to make decisions about whether to grant you credit, including mortgage lenders and credit card issuers.

Your credit ratings, such as the widely used FICO score, are also determined using the details of your credit history. The length of time credit accounts have been open and active, the patterns and regularity of payments over longer periods, as well as current activity, are all taken into consideration by creditors when reviewing your credit history. Your credit score is also influenced by your credit mix and credit utilization ratio.

A strong credit history demonstrates that you have paid your debts on time and do not have a lot of outstanding debt. You are a lower-risk borrower as a result. It's simpler to get authorized for loans and to receive cheaper interest rates when you have a strong credit history.

Paying off all of your debts in full each month is the greatest method to keep a decent credit rating. You should only have three or four credit cards at most, maintain your balances low on them for a long time, and never spend more than 30% of your available credit on any one card.

Additionally, be sure to aggressively repair any problems you uncover in your credit reports by routinely checking them.

Negative Credit History

On the other hand, folks with a terrible credit history often have debt that hasn't been paid off.

Late or missing payments, extensive credit card use, making several credit inquiries quickly, and experiencing significant financial calamities including bankruptcy, foreclosure, repossession, charge-offs, and settled accounts are all factors that might result in a poor credit history.

Low credit limits with high-interest rates, paying security deposits for items like mobile phones or apartment and vehicle rentals, and paying higher auto insurance premiums are all consequences of having bad credit.

A poor credit history may be fixed, but it will take time. You should examine your credit score often to determine which bad elements are most significant. You should also pay your payments on time, work off your credit card debt, and only occasionally apply for new credit.

Lack of Credit History

Young individuals who are college-age and have no credit history may find it challenging to be accepted for large loans or leases. If a prospective tenant has no credit history that proves their capacity to make timely payments, landlords may opt not to rent them an apartment.

Take out a modest personal loan or apply for a credit card with a low available amount to start building your credit history. Such use enables you to show, before taking on higher amounts of debt, how effectively you can manage your credit on a modest scale.

You may also obtain a secured credit card, which is secured by a sum of money that you deposit in a savings account, or a joint credit card with a person who has a solid credit history.

Particular Considerations

If you have paid off all of your bills and refrain from applying for a loan, credit card, or other type of financing for a while, you may be able to have a negative credit history erased. Seven or ten years are possible during this period. If such lengthy gaps exist, even consumers with strong past credit histories might essentially start again.

Chapter 3

Getting Around the Credit Landscape

Managing your finances and attaining your financial objectives may require you to navigate the credit environment. Your ability to acquire credit is important for many financial decisions you make, including receiving a credit card, a mortgage, a vehicle, or even a job in certain situations. The following are the essential actions and ideas to guide you through the credit landscape successfully:

Recognise Your Credit Score:

☐ Your credit score is a quantitative indicator of your creditworthiness. The two most popular credit rating formulas are VantageScore and FICO.
☐ The conditions of a loan may be more favorable if you have a credit score that is higher (often over 700).

Check Your Credit Report:

☐ Request free copies of your credit reports from each of the three main credit bureaus

(Equifax, Experian, and TransUnion) at least once each year.
- ☐ Check your credit reports for fraud, mistakes, or inaccurate information. Dispute any inconsistencies you discover.

Establish Credit:

- ☐ If you're just getting started with credit, think about getting a secured credit card or adding yourself as an authorized user on someone else's card.
- ☐ Build your credit history over time by paying your bills on time and keeping your credit utilization low.

Use Credit Responsibly:

- ☐ Pay your payments on time since your payment history affects your credit score significantly.
- ☐ Maintain modest credit card balances compared to your available credit (preferably around 30% utilization).
- ☐ Try to limit the number of credit accounts you open at once to avoid lowering your average account age.

Diversify Your Credit Mix:

☐ Possessing a variety of credit products (such as credit cards, installment loans, and mortgages) will help your credit score.

Manage Your Debt:

☐ Make a budget to successfully manage your money and prevent racking up excessive debt.
☐ Pay off high-interest obligations first, such as credit card bills, to save money on interest payments.

- Consider utilizing credit monitoring services to maintain tabs on changes to your credit record and to spot any possible fraud or identity theft.
- Avoid credit repair scams. Watch out for businesses that claim to "fix" your credit in exchange for money. You can raise your credit score on your own, and many of them are frauds.
- Know Your Rights: Become acquainted with the laws governing consumer rights and credit reporting, such as the Fair Credit Reporting Act (FCRA).

- Plan for Major Financial Milestones: Recognise how your credit score may affect your ability to get a car loan, mortgage, or other big loans. Aim to keep a high credit score to get better terms and interest rates.
- Seek Professional Advice When Needed: You may want to speak with a financial adviser or credit counselor if you're having trouble making ends meet or have complicated credit problems.
- Be Patient and Persistent: It takes time to establish and maintain excellent credit. Keep up your decent credit practices and be patient.

Your credit history is a long-term financial asset, so keep that in mind. Successfully navigating the credit environment demands constant attention and sound money management. You may keep or enhance your creditworthiness and make wise financial selections by comprehending the fundamental ideas and adopting proactive measures.

Various Forms of Business Credit

Similar to personal credit, business credit has many distinct forms and uses. Establishing and utilizing business credit may be crucial for your company's financial stability and growth. The following are some typical forms of business credit:

- **Business credit cards:** Although they resemble personal credit cards, business credit cards are intended for use only for company spending. You may use them to segregate your personal and corporate funds. These cards often include features like employee cards, spending monitoring, and incentive programs designed with company requirements in mind.
- Business Lines of Credit: A business line of credit gives you access to a certain amount of money that you may use as you need it. It is a flexible lending option for addressing short-term cash flow shortages since interest is often only applied to the amount borrowed.
- Business Loans: SBA (Small Business Administration) Loans, equipment loans, and term loans are just a few of the several types of business loans available. Term loans provide a one-time financial

infusion that must be repaid with interest over a certain period.

Loans for equipment are utilized just to buy equipment, and the equipment is often used as collateral. SBA loans are guaranteed by the government and created to help small companies. They often have better conditions and cheaper interest rates.

- Trade credit is an arrangement between a company and its vendors or suppliers to purchase products or services on credit terms. It enables a company to acquire products or services upfront and pay for them later, often within 30, 60, or 90 days.
- Invoice finance, also known as accounts receivable financing, enables a company to obtain a portion of the value of its outstanding bills upfront. When the invoice is due, the finance firm receives the entire amount of the invoice from the client after subtracting fees.
- Vendor Credit: Some suppliers and vendors may provide credit terms to companies with whom they have a long-standing commercial connection. This enables you to manage your cash flow as

you may obtain products or services before making a payment.

- Business credit ratings are produced for firms by business credit agencies including Dun & Bradstreet, Experian Business, and Equifax Business. These ratings determine how creditworthy your business is and might affect your capacity to get funding and good conditions.
- Commercial Real Estate Loans: You may apply for commercial real estate loans, which are specially made for this purpose, if your company wants to buy or lease commercial real estate.
- Business Charge Cards: These cards resemble credit cards in many ways, but you normally have to pay the amount in full each month. They provide spending freedom without accumulating debt, which is advantageous for companies with predictable cash flow.
- Merchant cash advances: In return for a portion of your daily credit card sales, merchant cash advances provide up-front financing. A predetermined portion of future credit card transactions is used to make repayments.

It's crucial for company owners to appropriately manage their business credit and have a good credit history. An efficient business credit profile may assist you in obtaining finance, negotiating better supplier conditions, and expanding your company.

Deciding on the Best Credit Products

Whether you're an individual searching for personal credit or a company owner looking for commercial credit, choosing the correct credit product is an important financial choice. You can reach your financial objectives and manage your debt responsibly with the correct credit package. The following are things to think about while selecting the best credit product:

Identify Your Financial Goals:

- Identify the precise reason why you need financing. Is it for a significant purchase, debt relief, managing financial flow, or something else?
- Your credit product decision will be influenced by your financial objectives. For instance, a mortgage is appropriate for property purchases, but a personal loan could be preferable for debt consolidation.

Evaluate Your Financial Situation:

- ☐ Examine your present financial situation, taking into account your income, spending, outstanding debt, and credit rating.
- ☐ Knowing your financial condition will enable you to choose the form of credit that you can both afford and qualify for.

Research Credit Products That Are Available:

- ☐ Investigate the many credit options, such as personal loans, credit cards, home equity loans, business lines of credit, etc.
- ☐ Recognise the characteristics, conditions, interest rates, and costs related to each form of credit instrument.

Compare Interest Rates:

- ☐ Interest rates have a big influence on how much money you have to borrow overall. Comparing the interest rates provided by various lenders or credit card companies.
- ☐ Pay attention to whether the rates are variable (may fluctuate over time) or fixed (stay constant).

Take into Account the Repayment Periods:

- Repayment periods for various loan programs vary. For instance, although personal loans have set monthly installment payments, credit cards allow for minimum monthly payments.
- Pick a payback period that works with your spending plan and financial objectives.
- Examine the costs related to the credit product, such as yearly fees, origination fees, late payment fees, and debt transfer fees.
- When determining the total cost of the credit, take these costs into account.

Understanding Credit Limits or Loan Amount

- Check to see whether the credit limit or loan amount you're qualified for satisfies your borrowing requirements.
- Remember that reaching your credit limit to the maximum will lower your credit score.

Verify Your Credit Eligibility

- Some credit products may have unique eligibility requirements, such as credit score requirements and proof of income.
- Check your credit score to see whether you fulfill the requirements of the lender.

Evaluate Risk and Security

- Consider whether the credit product is secured or unsecured when evaluating risk and security.
- Compared to unsecured loans or credit products, secured loans or credit products need collateral.
- Be aware of the effects a credit default will have on your assets and credit score.

Examine the Small Print

- Carefully read the credit product's terms and conditions, including the small print.
- Pay close attention to any limits or limitations, penalty clauses, or changes in interest rates.

Seek Expert Advice

☐ When in doubt about the best credit product for you or if you have complicated financial requirements, consider speaking with a financial adviser or credit counselor.

Plan for Repayment

☐ Create a repayment plan before you take out credit to be sure you can fulfill your financial commitments and appropriately pay off the debt.

Keep in mind that picking the correct credit product might affect your financial situation for years to come. Spend some time finding, comparing, and choosing the credit package that best suits your financial objectives and capabilities.

Credit Reporting Organisations and Ratings

In the financial world, credit reporting agencies and credit ratings are essential since they evaluate and communicate your creditworthiness. They are crucial in determining how well you can handle your credit and financial obligations for lenders, renters, and other parties. An overview of credit reporting companies and credit ratings is provided below:

Credit reporting agencies, sometimes known as credit bureaus:

Equifax

1. One of the three main credit reporting companies in the United States is Equifax.
2. It compiles and keeps track of consumer and company credit data.
3. Both people and corporations may get credit reports and ratings from Equifax.

Experian

1. One of the three main credit reporting companies is Experian.
2. It collects and retains credit information on both people and companies.
3. Experian provides some credit-related services, including credit reports and ratings.

TransUnion

1. TransUnion, the third largest credit reporting agency, gathers and maintains credit data on both individuals and companies.
2. Both people and corporations may get credit reports and ratings from TransUnion.

These credit reporting companies gather and preserve data on your credit history, including information about your credit accounts, payment history, unpaid amounts, and public records (including bankruptcies and tax liens). These organizations get frequent reports from lenders and creditors with this information.

Credit Scores

FICO Score

1. One of the most popular credit scoring algorithms in the US is the FICO Score.
2. Many lenders use it to evaluate credit risk; it was created by the Fair Isaac Corporation.
3. FICO scores vary from 300 to 850; higher scores indicate more creditworthiness.

4. There are several FICO Scores designed for various forms of financing, such as mortgages and car loans.

VantageScore

1. A second well-liked credit scoring methodology that evaluates credit risk is VantageScore.
2. Equifax, Experian, and TransUnion, the three main credit reporting organizations, created it.
3. VantageScores are another scoring system that ranges from 300 to 850, with higher scores indicating more creditworthiness.
4. Many lenders utilize VantageScore in addition to or in substitute for FICO Scores.

How Credit Scores Are Calculated:

Your credit report's data is used to compute your credit score. The precise formulae employed by FICO and VantageScore are confidential and not made public, however, the main elements that often affect your credit score are as follows:

1. Payment history, including on-timeliness of bill payments.
2. Amounts outstanding, including loan and credit card debt.
3. Credit history (the length of time you have had credit accounts).
4. Credit mix (types of credit accounts, including installment loans, mortgages, and credit cards).
5. New credit queries, or recent credit applications.

Credit Score Importance

Because they enable lenders to determine the risk of lending to you, credit ratings are crucial. A higher credit score generally indicates that you are a less hazardous borrower, which may lead to cheaper interest rates and better loan conditions. Furthermore, having good credit is essential for:

1. Renting a house or a flat.

2. Being eligible for insurance coverage.
3. Having access to utility services.
4. In certain circumstances, finding work.
5. Receiving approval for loans and credit cards.

Checking your credit reports from the main credit reporting agencies regularly is crucial to verify accuracy and keep track of your credit history. You may contest any mistakes to get them fixed if you find any. To reach your financial objectives and get inexpensive financing when you need it, you must build and maintain strong credit.

Chapter 4

The Application Procedure

Applications for business credit are essential for helping firms analyze and manage credit risk because, if used properly, they may help you find organizations with whom you wish to exercise caution when granting credit. Most businesses don't utilize business credit applications, and even those that don't follow up with them after they've been completed or request the extra information needed to fully comprehend the risk involved, do they?

Preparing for a Credit Application

To increase your chances of acceptance and get favorable conditions, you must prepare for credit applications. Applying for a credit card, personal loan, mortgage, or any other sort of credit? These steps may help you get ready:

- Check Your Credit Reports: Request free copies of your credit reports from Equifax, Experian, and TransUnion, the three main credit reporting agencies. Check your credit reports for fraud, mistakes, and inconsistencies.

Challenge any errors you discover to make sure your credit reports are correct.

- Recognise Your Credit Score: Recognise your credit score from each of the three main credit agencies since various lenders may use different scores.

Recognise the elements that affect your credit score and how to raise it if required.

- Reduce Outstanding Debt: Work on bringing down your credit card balances and paying off any high-interest bills. You may improve your credit score by lowering your debt-to-credit ratio (credit utilization).
- Pay Bills on Time: Keep paying all of your debts and credit card responsibilities on time. Your credit score may suffer significantly as a result of late payments.
- Avoid New Credit Inquiries: Reduce the amount of credit inquiries you make in the months before your significant credit application. A sudden increase in credit inquiries may temporarily reduce your credit score.
- Review Your Finances: Determine if you can easily handle additional credit by evaluating your present financial condition. To establish how much you can afford to borrow and return, create a budget.
- Compile Required Documents: Various credit application types may call for particular paperwork, including identification evidence, tax records, bank statements, and proof of income. Have

these papers available to provide when the lender requests them.

- Examine Offers and Lenders: Examine offers from several lenders to see which one best meets your requirements. Take into account the interest rates, costs, credit limitations, payback schedule, and any unique features or benefits.
- Prequalify if Possible: Prequalification, which some lenders provide, enables you to determine your likelihood of approval without a rigorous credit investigation, which is a good idea. It might assist you in narrowing your search to lenders who are more likely to accept your application.
- Read and Understand the Terms: Thoroughly go through the terms and conditions of the credit product you're applying for. Recognise the fees, interest rate, repayment plan, and any penalties.
- Get Ready for a Credit Check: Recognise that the majority of credit applications include a rigorous credit check, which

may momentarily reduce your credit score. Do not apply for credit unless you need it and have a good chance of getting it.

- Consider Co-Signers or Collateral: If your credit isn't good enough to qualify you for the credit product you want, you may require a co-signer or collateral (for secured loans) to increase your chances of acceptance.
- There is always a potential for rejection, so have a plan in case it happens. Don't get upset if your application is rejected. Before reapplying, find out why your application was denied specifically by the lender and focus on raising your credit score.
- Apply strategically since timing is important when applying for credit. When your finances are secure and your credit is strong, apply.

Making an Effective Business Plan

The foundation for success is laid by a solid business strategy, nothing more. The act of constructing one not only defines your objectives and highlights possible difficulties but also aids in attracting investors and strategic partners.

Typically, a business plan has seven sections: an executive summary;

1. Executive summary
2. A description of the company
3. A market study
4. A description of the product or service
5. Sales and marketing strategy
6. An organizational and management structure
7. Financial Projection

We asked business professionals to give their tips on writing an effective business plan to help you get started. Their top six tactics are shown here.

- Start with the fundamentals.

Tim Berry, founder and chairman of Palo Alto Software, which offers launch and management tools for small businesses, advises breaking down your idea into digestible chunks. You might start by writing bullet points and then elaborate on them.

Start with the fundamentals: your company plan, the methods you'll use to carry it out, and important dates like launch dates. Determine your best predictions for revenue in the first several months and include initial expenditures such as inventory, equipment, and permits. You can figure out how much money you'll need by looking at your finances.

- Keep your audience in mind

According to Akira Hirai, founder, and CEO of Cayenne Consulting, a business plan consulting company, if you wish to pitch investors, your plan should show that you have a better product or service that resolves a challenging issue for a large target market. If you want to attract a strategic partner, your plan—which is often included with a partnership proposal—should outline your vision and capacity to assist the partner in achieving its strategic objectives.

Make the argument that your founding team has the knowledge and abilities to create a successful firm, says Hirai, regardless of who you are creating your strategy for. A short biography of the founders, including their job experience, education, and background as it relates to your company, should be included in the description of your organizational and managerial structure.

- Put expansion ahead of profits.

According to Berry, "startup founders frequently create wildly improbable projections because they believe investors want to see profits." Such figures, however, won't be taken seriously by investors, and they may also be seen as a lack of focus on growth on the part of the entrepreneur.

"There's a tradeoff between profits and growth since growth comes from spending," Berry, an angel investor as well, continues. "You'll have trouble generating growth if you have too much profit," Explaining how your company will expand should be your main concern.

- Establish a stable financial flow

Your anticipated cash flow, planned revenues and costs, and other financial information should all be fully disclosed in the business plan's financial section. Regardless of how good your concept is, failing to prepare for the timing of financial inflows and withdrawals can leave your company open to failure. Berry asserts, "You can't just run out of money." You put yourself at risk if you don't prepare for and manage cash flow.

Make careful to accurately estimate the costs and profits of your business. Certain costs are simple to forget, such as merchant services fees and various kinds of insurance. If you forecast your costs using a cash flow template, be sure to include all of your spending categories.

- Keep it pristine

Hirai feels that beauty is important. "A well-designed plan that is attractive and well-formatted is more likely to be read than a disjointed plan."

Investors often like executive summaries that are one to three pages long and comprehensive plans that are 20 to 25 pages long. Plans with grammatical or spelling errors, as well as those that are dense with technical information or scientific jargon, may be rejected.

- Examine and update your plan.

Some company owners finish a strategy, put it away, and never look at it again. Berry advises that you review your strategy every month to ensure that you are on track to achieve your goals and to compare your predictions with reality. "All of that review creates real management and accountability," he asserts. Additionally, it enables you to change directions rapidly if sales, market circumstances, or other things don't pan out as planned.

Filling out an Outstanding Credit Application

A credit application is what.

A credit application is the official request for a credit extension made by a borrower to a lender. Credit applications may be submitted electronically, verbally, or in writing. The application must include every piece of data the lender needs to decide whether to approve it, whether it is delivered in person or not. Following the law, credit applicants also have the right to fair treatment.

KEY TAKEAWAYS

1. A credit application is a way for prospective borrowers to ask lenders for money or access to it.
2. Nowadays, credit applications may often be filed online and may be accepted quickly.
3. Laws that protect borrowers from discrimination and other unfair lending practices control the credit application procedure.

On a credit application, what questions are there?

When you apply for credit, you will have to respond to a series of inquiries and, often, provide supporting evidence. This data is used by the lender to assess how dangerous or safe it would be to grant your request.

The Consumer Financial Protection Bureau states that the following information is likely to be requested, however, applications may vary somewhat based on the kind of loan and the lender:

1. Documentation of any name change, if recent

2. Proof of your identification (such as a driver's license or other formal ID)
3. Your Social Security number
4. Your pay stubs from the previous 30 days
5. W-2 forms from the previous two years
6. Your signed federal income tax returns from the last two years
7. Proof of any other sources of income you may have
8. The two most recent bank statements.

If Your Application Is Rejected, What to Do?

You have a right to be informed of the reasons why your credit application was denied. The lender will often explain the reasons in what is legally known as an adverse action letter that is sent to you. If your credit score was too low, for instance, it must provide you with your score and the date it was reported.

If you'd like, you may get in touch with the lender and urge it to think again, perhaps in light of the fresh facts you might provide. Of course, you may also just switch lenders.

An unfavorable action letter could help highlight your credit's weak points so you can strengthen them before reapplying.

Chapter 5

Managing and Using Business Credit

Running a firm without money severely reduces your ability to compete, leaving you vulnerable to any catastrophe. Money was scarce when I launched my business because of a terrible recession. The business expanded as the economy improved, but I was unable to go as far as I had hoped to until I had access to real cash in the form of loans.

While you could overlook investment-required prospects, your competitors plow forward, gaining market share. Sadly, maintaining a strong expenditure account is insufficient to maintain an advantage. One of your most valuable assets is your company's credit history since it gives you access to better leasing terms and loans while guaranteeing that resources are used impartially.

Without money, crises simply cannot be overcome, yet debt itself may result in disaster. Credit should thus not be used to generate static debt, but rather to appropriately manage existing debt to have a spotless credit history. Payments must be paid on time or 30 days before their due date.

A thorough credit profile will provide customers and investors with essential information when they look into your company's reputation.

Use of Credit Responsibly

For preserving sound financial standing and a strong credit history, responsible credit utilization is essential. Credit may help you reach your financial objectives and establish a solid credit record when utilized responsibly. Here are some essential guidelines for using credit responsibly:

- Pay Your Expenses on Time: One of the most important aspects of keeping excellent credit is consistently making on-time payments for credit cards, loans, and other expenses. Late fines, increased interest rates, and credit score loss may all result from missed payments.
- Use Credit Sparingly: Steer clear of going into debt for more than you can reasonably handle. A good rule of thumb for maintaining a healthy credit utilization

ratio is to keep your credit card balances below 30% of your credit limit.

- Create and Stick to a Budget: Create a budget to keep tabs on your earnings and outgoings. This will assist you in managing your money well and save you from taking on further debt. Incorporate a strategy for paying off current obligations.
- Pay More Than the Minimum Due: When you have credit card debt, strive to make a larger payment each month than the minimum. A lengthier repayment time and greater interest rates may come from making just the minimal payment.
- Avoid Closing Old Accounts: Your credit score is influenced by the duration of your credit history. Your credit history will likely be shortened if you close old accounts, which might reduce your score. Even if you just sometimes use your older accounts, keep them open and current.
- Regularly Monitor Your Credit: At the very least once a year, check the credit reports from all three main credit agencies. You may find inaccuracies, contest them, and spot any indications of identity theft by keeping an eye on your credit.

- Be Careful with Credit Inquiries: Each hard credit query (such as applying for a new credit card or loan) will temporarily reduce your credit score. Do not apply for credit frequently, and only when necessary.
- Diversify Your Credit Mix: Having a variety of credit accounts, including mortgages, credit cards, and installment loans, might help your credit score. Open new accounts, though, only when you truly need them and are capable of handling them responsibly.
- Read and comprehend the terms and conditions of your credit agreements, including the interest rates, fees, and payment deadlines. Know any fines for late payments or going above credit limits.
- Plan for Financial Emergencies: Have an emergency fund ready to pay for unforeseen costs so you won't have to depend on credit cards. Refrain from utilizing credit as a long-term fix for your money problems.
- Educate Yourself About Credit: Keep up with financial literacy and credit-related issues to make wise choices about how to use and handle credit.

Tracking Your Credit Profile

To preserve the accuracy of your credit information, safeguard against identity theft, and keep your credit in good standing, you must regularly monitor your credit profile. For successful credit profile monitoring, use these procedures and ideas:

- Regularly check your credit reports:
1. Request free copies of your credit reports at least once each year from each of the three main credit agencies (Equifax, Experian, and TransUnion).
2. The sole authorized provider of free yearly credit reports is AnnualCreditReport.com, where you may obtain these reports.
- Review Your Credit Reports Thoroughly:
1. Carefully review the correctness of your credit reports. Search for any inconsistencies, mistakes, or fake accounts.
2. Make sure no names or addresses are misspelled, and make sure no accounts are strange.
- Dispute Mistakes Quickly:

1. File a dispute with the credit bureaus if you find any inaccuracies or anomalies on your credit reports.
2. To back up your claim, provide evidence, and then check back to make sure the adjustments were done.

- Consider Credit Monitoring Services:

1. Credit monitoring services may provide you with real-time notifications when anything changes on your credit reports, enabling you to quickly spot questionable behavior.
2. Although there may be a cost associated with these services, they may be beneficial for continuous credit protection.

- Set Up Fraud warnings: Ask the credit bureaus to place fraud warnings. These warnings advise creditors to use more vigilance when confirming your identification before granting credit. Fraud alerts may last up to a year and are free.

- Think about a credit freeze (security freeze):

1. An identity thief will find it difficult to create new accounts in your name since a credit freeze limits access to your credit reports.

2. When you need to apply for credit, you may temporarily remove the freeze. Your credit may incur fees if it is frozen and then thawed.

- Check your bank and credit card statements:

1. Consistently check your bank and credit card statements for unauthorized or unusual activities.
2. Inform your banking institutions right away of any inconsistencies.

- Protect Personal Information:

1. Preserve your financial and personal data. Share private information with care, particularly over the phone and online.
2. For online accounts, use strong, one-time passwords, and where two-factor authentication is an option, think about utilizing it.

- Watch Out for Phishing Scams:

1. Exercise caution when responding to emails, messages, or phone calls that ask for personal or financial information.
2. Make immediate contact with the organization via the appropriate procedures to confirm the authenticity of any request.

- Monitor Your Credit Scores:

1. Check your credit scores regularly since they provide you with an overview of how your credit is doing.
2. Credit ratings are freely accessible via several credit card providers and credit monitoring services.
- Report Lost or Stolen Documents: Contact the appropriate law enforcement agencies and financial institutions right away if your identity or credit cards are lost or stolen.
- Educate Yourself About Identity Theft: To identify possible dangers and respond appropriately, be knowledgeable about identity theft and prevalent scams.

Increasing Credit Limit

Increasing your credit lines, whether via credit cards or other sources of credit, has several advantages, including the ability to borrow more money and perhaps raising your credit score. To prevent overextending yourself financially or damaging your credit, it's crucial to handle this procedure cautiously.

Increasing your credit lines, whether via credit cards or other sources of credit, has some advantages, including the ability to borrow more money and perhaps raising your credit score. To prevent overextending yourself financially or damaging your credit, it's crucial to handle this procedure cautiously. Following are some suggestions for responsible credit line expansion:

1. Evaluate Your Financial Situation: Before applying for more credit, consider how your finances are currently faring. Make sure you can properly handle any new debt without going overboard.
2. Verify Your Credit Reports and Score: Review your credit reports from the three main credit agencies to make sure they are correct and current. To determine your creditworthiness, check your credit score. Your chances of being approved might increase with a better score.
3. Understand Your Credit Goals: Specify your goals for increasing your credit lines. Are you trying to raise your credit score, finance a significant purchase, or cut costs more effectively?

4. Consider several credit options, including credit cards, personal loans, home equity lines of credit (HELOCs), and business lines of credit, based on your circumstances.

5. Review Existing Credit Accounts: Examine your current credit accounts, including loans and credit cards, to see if you can raise the credit limits on any of them. Ask your creditors if they may raise your credit limit by getting in touch with them. Prepare an explanation for the request, such as evidence of solid payment history and prudent credit utilization.

6. Use Caution while Applying for New Credit: Avoid creating too many new credit accounts quickly since doing so might temporarily reduce your credit score due to repeated credit queries. Only apply for more credit if you need it and are capable of handling it properly.

7. Use Secured Credit Cards (if necessary): If your credit history is sketchy or you have bad credit, you may want to apply for a secured credit card. Secured cards demand a security deposit but may aid in credit repair or building. Verify that the issuer sends information about your

payment history to the main credit reporting agencies.

8. Use credit responsibly by making on-time payments on all of your credit accounts. Your credit score is greatly influenced by your payment history. Maintain low credit card balances in comparison to your available credit (target for a utilization rate of 30%).

9. Keep a Variety of Credit Accounts: Having a variety of credit accounts, including credit cards, installment loans, and mortgages, may help your credit score. Be careful not to have too many accounts of the same kind.

10. Monitor Your Credit: Keep tabs on the correctness of your credit reports and scores as well as any unauthorized or questionable activity.

11. Use Credit Limit Increases Wisely: If your credit limit is raised, make good use of it. Avoid spending too much money or taking on unneeded debt. Keep in mind that just because your credit limit is bigger doesn't imply you should spend more.

12. Pay Close Attention to Fees and Conditions: Carefully go through all of the terms and conditions of new credit

accounts, including interest rates, yearly fees, and any promotional times. Recognise the effects the credit conditions will have on your entire financial status.

When done with consideration and responsibility, credit line expansion may be a useful financial instrument. It may assist you in reaching your financial objectives and enhancing your creditworthiness; yet, to safeguard your financial security, it's essential to refrain from taking on more debt than you can handle and to practice excellent credit practices.

Chapter 6

Strategies for Growth and Prosperity

Every entrepreneur wants to succeed in the cutthroat business environment of today. However, achieving company success may be difficult and calls for a well-thought-out plan. We will examine tried-and-true tactics and crucial guidelines in this post to assist you in achieving outstanding company accomplishments.

- Having Specific Goals

The first step to success in a company is to clearly define your objectives. Set SMART (specific, measurable, attainable, relevant, and time-bound) objectives for both the short and long term. You may create targeted tactics to attain your goals by having a clear picture of what you want to accomplish.

- How to Write a Good Business Plan

A well-written company strategy serves as a success road map. Describe your goals, target market, competition analysis, marketing plans, projected finances, and growth methods. Review and update your company strategy often to account for changing market conditions and new possibilities.

- Creating a Powerful Team

A capable and driven workforce is essential to a company's success. Create a productive workplace, provide training and career possibilities, develop teamwork, and hire people with the appropriate talents and values. Innovation, productivity, and customer pleasure may all be fostered by a good team.

- Providing Exceptional Goods and/or Services

Concentrate on providing great goods or services if you want to stand out from the crowd. Recognize the demands of your consumers, recurrently enhance your offers, and surpass their expectations. Giving customers a memorable experience will increase their loyalty and encourage favorable word-of-mouth referrals.

- Using Successful Marketing Techniques

Create a thorough marketing plan that focuses on your ideal clients. Make use of a combination of online and offline platforms, including social media, content marketing, SEO, email marketing, and conventional advertising. To maximize outcomes, continuously track and evaluate your marketing initiatives.

- Promoting Creativity and Adaptability

Maintaining an advantage in the corporate world requires innovation. Encourage a culture of innovation and constant development. Keep up with industry trends, adopt new technology, and show flexibility in your company strategy to accommodate shifting consumer expectations.

- Putting Customer Satisfaction First

Long-term success depends on putting the needs of your clients first. Exceptional customer service, proactive feedback-seeking, and fast customer-reporting are all required. Develop a solid rapport with your consumers since happy customers are more likely to recommend your business to others.

- Keeping Your Financial Health

To continue your firm, use good financial management practices. Track your cash flow, make smart financial decisions, and stick to your budget. Analyze your financial accounts regularly, get help from a professional when necessary, and make development and investment plans for the future.

- **Credit for Business Growth**

Over the last three years, owners of small businesses have faced significant economic challenges. In addition to surviving a pandemic, they have had to deal with historically high borrowing rates, inflation, a shaky supply chain, and a tight employment market. Enough said about how resilient small company entrepreneurs are.

Fortunately, it seems like 2023 will be a better year. Almost half of small company owners (49%) and global business owners (45%) expressed confidence in the economy. In the next year, they anticipate increasing sales and revenue, which will result in bigger profits and more substantial expenditures to support the expansion of the firm. Compared to more conventional sources of finance like company loans, the advantages and incentives offered by business credit cards provide special benefits for expanding and developing a corporation.

- **Developing a Plan to Find and Keep Talent**

The challenge of hiring has never been greater for small company owners. While companies of all sizes face difficulties as a result of the current labor market, small firms are disproportionately affected since they sometimes lack the capital on hand required to provide competitive pay or benefit packages.

By using credit cards and the cash back and benefits they provide, business owners may reduce their spending and free up funds for hiring and retaining great employees. Fast-growing businesses, like Mvnifest, are expanding so rapidly that every dollar they earn is reinvested in the firm.

Business credit might provide chances to invest in fostering a positive company culture since there is a significant correlation between content workers and a successful company. To thank their staff, small company owners could think about utilizing the points on their cards to buy gift cards. Others could think about utilizing their travel incentives to organize team retreats and get-togethers for their remote personnel.

- **Inventory Purchases to Counter Inflationary Pressures**

For company owners, who almost universally (94%) think inflation has affected expenditures, the growing cost of supplies is creating an increasingly difficult situation. Business owners must weather the inevitable ups and downs of that supply chain, whether they are caused by seasonality or inflation, to secure long-term success.

Using a business credit card to pre-purchase inventory and acquire essential supplies can help business owners prepare for sudden growth opportunities. This method enables contractors and manufacturers to react to buy orders more confidently without worrying that supply chain problems will scuttle a good transaction. It also locks company owners into existing, known margins throughout an unpredictable inflationary climate.

Purchasing inventory has the potential to generate financial savings since wholesalers sometimes offer goods in large quantities at reduced costs. This consistency is a huge competitive advantage in an economic environment that is constantly changing.

- Making Connections While Travelling for Business

Success often brings with it the potential for development into new target areas, which necessitates additional business travel. Business owners may attend in-person pitches or sales meetings, visit with manufacturing partners, or check out potential retail locations using the travel advantages offered by their business credit cards.

While maintaining contact with customers and suppliers may be a benefit of business travel, in the post-pandemic employment market, it has also become crucial for fostering camaraderie among distant teams. Business travel—for both employees and business leaders—will continue to be crucial when it comes to establishing the team connectivity that will foster ongoing growth, according to the majority (52%) of survey respondents in our 2023 Business Leaders Outlook.

- Streamlining Financial Procedures Through Automation

Tools that automate financial business procedures are important to entrepreneurs because they save time, cut down on mistakes, and boost productivity. Accounting software and programs provide company owners the ability to receive payments from customers, manage and pay bills, and start the payroll process all via one simple system.

Similar to this, simplifying financial service providers speeds up timeframes, streamlines accounting, and minimizes human tasks. Business owners are increasingly searching for a financial solution that includes business banking, business credit, and business payments, like Chase for Business.

By doing this, company owners may make no-fee, same-day deposits and have access to their money as soon as feasible. Additionally, it gives users access to value-added services like Customer Insights, which provides companies with performance information to help them engage consumers more effectively and manage their finances.

Making Smart Investment with Business Credit

When someone defines themselves as "in debt," it's sometimes seen as a bad sign; they may have overused their credit card or may otherwise be having financial difficulties. The debt that results from taking out a small company loan or a line of credit facility, however, may, under the appropriate conditions, be a step towards development for certain small business owners.

Using business credit properly might aid in the expansion and monetary objectives of your company. To prevent financial hazards, it is crucial to handle company financing effectively and carefully. Here are some pointers for making effective use of company credit investments:

1. Set Specific Investment Goals: Before using a company loan, specify your investment goals. Establish your goals, whether they be to increase your operations, buy equipment, introduce a new product, or improve cash flow.
2. Make a Thorough Business Plan: Create a thorough business plan that details your financial estimates, investment plans, and objectives. A well-structured strategy may aid in decision-making by allowing you to

analyze the prospective return on investment.

3. Build a Solid Business Credit Profile: Create and enhance your company's credit profile by utilizing credit wisely. This entails handling credit responsibly and paying payments on time. Securing funding with favorable conditions may be simpler if your firm has a good credit history.

4. Select the Proper Credit Product: Decide which credit product best suits your demands for investments. company credit lines, company credit cards, and equipment finance are among the available options. Take into account elements like interest rates, periods of repayment, and the goal of the loan product.

5. Negotiate Favourable Conditions: When looking for company finance, haggle conditions and interest rates with lenders to get the best deals. Strong creditworthiness and a well-thought-out company strategy may aid in better conditions being negotiated.

6. Utilise Credit for Profitability and Growth: Use your company credit to fund

projects that will probably result in returns and boost profitability. Refrain from utilizing company credit for unnecessary expenditures or uncertain business projects.

7. Managing the Budget and Cash Flow: Create a budget that takes your credit repayment responsibilities into account. Make sure your cash flow can cover operational costs as well as debt repayment.

8. Spread Out Your Investments: Refrain from investing all of your borrowed money in a single asset or venture. Your assets may help spread risk by becoming more diverse. To balance liquidity and growth potential, take into account a combination of short-term and long-term investments.

9. Observe Your Investments: Monitor the performance of your investments regularly to judge their success and make necessary modifications. Be ready to adjust your investing approach if the market situation changes.

10. Repayment Strategy: Create a detailed repayment strategy for your company credit, taking into account both interest

and principal installments. Making timely payments is essential for preserving a good credit history.

11. Think about Professional Counsel: If you're unsure about managing company credit or making investment choices, speak with financial advisers or business consultants who have experience in your sector.

12. Prepare for Unforeseen Difficulties: Create backup strategies for dealing with unforeseen setbacks or changes in the corporate environment. Sufficient cash reserves may assist you in overcoming unanticipated difficulties.

13. Review the Tax Ramifications: Recognise how your investments' tax consequences may affect your entire financial situation. Speak with a tax professional to improve your tax planning.

Using business credit correctly may help your company grow, but doing so calls for careful planning and sound money management. You may use business credit as an effective instrument for development and success by matching your credit utilization to your company's objectives and upholding responsible credit practices.

Lowering Credit Risks

A crucial component of controlling financial risk for both lenders and borrowers is credit risk mitigation. Credit risk is the possibility of financial loss brought on by a borrower's inability to pay back a loan or fulfill other credit obligations. The following are tips and tactics for reducing credit risk:

1. Credit Evaluation and Analysis: Thoroughly evaluate prospective borrowers' creditworthiness. This entails assessing their cash flow, debt capacity, credit history, and financial documents. To evaluate creditworthiness, use credit scoring algorithms and credit records.

2. Diversification: Diversify your portfolio of credit by making loans to a range of borrowers or investing in a range of asset classes. Spreading your credit exposure may assist in lessening the effects of individual borrowers' or industries' failures.

3. Ratios of Loan-to-Value: (LTV)Keep proper LTV ratios for loans with collateral, such as mortgages or vehicle loans. A cushion against a drop in the value of the collateral is provided by a lower LTV ratio. Regularly assess collateral values to make sure they are still sufficient.

4. Covenants and Guarantees for Loans: Incorporate protective covenants into loan agreements that impose obligations on borrowers to follow particular risk-reduction guidelines or satisfy certain financial benchmarks. Take into account the need for individual or corporate guarantees, particularly for debtors with greater risk.

5. Stress Examinations: Run stress tests to see how your credit portfolio would fare in a downturn in the economy. This analysis aids in identifying weaknesses

and equips you to weather economic downturns.

6. Regular Observations: Throughout the credit period, keep a close eye on your borrowers' financial situation. Install early detection systems to look for indications of financial crisis.

7. Credit Ceilings and Exposure Control: Determine credit limits for certain counterparties or borrowers based on their risk and creditworthiness characteristics. Use exposure limits to control the risk of concentration in your portfolio.

8. Pricing Based on Risk: Modify conditions and interest rates per the credit risk posed by the borrower. Higher interest rates and harsher restrictions should be applied to higher-risk borrowers.

9. Insurance for Credit and Derivative: When making high-risk loans or investments, think about getting credit insurance to guard against borrower defaults. To protect yourself from credit risk, use derivatives like credit default swaps.

10. Allowance for Credit Losses (Reserve for Loan Losses): Keep enough loan loss reserves in your portfolio to meet

anticipated credit losses. Based on your exposure to credit risk, evaluate and modify this reserve regularly.

11. Planning for Recovery from Default: Create a plan for reclaiming property or security in the event of a default. Make sure your procedure for handling late-paying customers is clear.

12. Risk Culture and Education: Encourage a robust risk management culture inside your company. Make sure every employee is aware of the significance of credit risk reduction. Offer continuing credit risk management training and education.

13. Observing Regulations: Maintain awareness of relevant laws and rules and abide by them. Risk management recommendations and capital adequacy norms are two examples of regulatory requirements.

14. Scenario Evaluation: Use scenario analysis to determine how different economic, market, or sector-specific events could affect your credit portfolio. Make wise judgments on risk management using the newfound knowledge.

Prudent lending techniques, successful risk management techniques, and continuing monitoring are all necessary components of the ongoing process of mitigating credit risk. By putting these safeguards in place, borrowers and financial institutions may lower their exposure to credit risk and improve their financial stability.

Chapter 7

Real-World Success Stories

Real-world success stories of people who have successfully used business credit may undoubtedly provide insightful information on how ethical credit management can support entrepreneurship. Here are a few motivational instances:

- **Benjamin Kapelushnik (Benjamin Kickz)**

Benjamin Kapelushnik, commonly known as Benjamin Kickz, is a young businessman who has created a successful company focused on trainers and streetwear. He began by buying limited-edition trainers and reselling them for a profit using his own money and company credit. By carefully managing his company credit, Benjamin was able to grow his firm, increase his inventory, and cultivate a devoted clientele. He is referred to in the industry as the "Sneaker Don" and his company, Sneaker Don, has grown into a multimillion-dollar operation.

- **Lisa Price (Carol's Daughter)**

Lisa Price started Carol's Daughter in her Brooklyn kitchen. Carol's Daughter is a beauty and haircare brand. She borrowed money from a small business lender and used her funds to start her company. Over time, Lisa developed her brand with the help of smart alliances and business credit. Carol's Daughter became well-known, and Lisa finally sold her business to L'Oréal, achieving notable success in the cosmetics business.

- **Evan Spiegel and Bobby Murphy (Snap Inc.)**

Evan Spiegel and Bobby Murphy, the co-founders of Snapchat and subsequently Snap Inc., obtained money via investments and venture capital. They took advantage of commercial credit lines to finance the organization's quick growth.

After becoming a publicly traded business in 2017, Snap Inc. now has a portfolio of goods outside Snapchat, such as Spectacles and advances in augmented reality.

- **Maria Contreras-Sweet (Promérica Bank)**

Maria Contreras-Sweet, a seasoned businesswoman and former head of the U.S. Small Business Administration (SBA), was instrumental in turning a faltering bank into a flourishing financial organization.

To rescue and expand Promérica Bank and ensure its continuing prosperity while serving underprivileged areas in California, Contreras-Sweet employed corporate credit methods and financial restructuring.

- **Daymond John (FUBU)**

Daymond John, a businessman in the fashion industry and star of the television series "Shark Tank," created the apparel line FUBU with the help of a modest business loan and donations from his own money. He extended the brand's reach through business finance and finally attained significant distribution agreements. As a result of FUBU's popularity as a worldwide fashion sensation, Daymond John has had a successful business career.

These real-world success stories show how smart use of business financing, together with creativity, tenacity, and a focused vision, may result in entrepreneurial success. It's crucial to remember that obtaining and maintaining company success depends on prudent credit management and financial restraint.

Case Studies of Business Credit Triumphs

Business credit successes often entail businesses employing credit wisely to meet their financial objectives, develop their operations, and get through difficult situations. Here are a few examples of companies that effectively used company loans as leverage:

- **Amazon**

The world's largest online retailer uses business finance to drive its explosive development. Amazon initially struggled with profitability as it made significant investments in growth and innovation. Amazon was able to fund its operations and create a sizable distribution network by obtaining loans and credit lines. One of the biggest merchants in the world, the firm saw enormous growth and profitability throughout time.

- **Ford Motor Company**

Henry Ford formed the Ford Motor Company, which revolutionized the vehicle industry by combining commercial credit and creative finance methods.

Ford introduced the assembly line and used company credit lines to finance manufacturing, greatly lowering production costs. Ford was able to increase the affordability of cars because of this, which helped them gain market domination.

- **Facebook**

The social media behemoth has financed its quick development and acquisitions via a variety of commercial credit products. This involves opening credit lines and issuing bonds for businesses. Through the use of these financial techniques, Facebook was able to invest in infrastructure, buy businesses like Instagram and WhatsApp, and maintain its position as the leader in the digital sector.

- **Starbucks**

The well-known international coffee giant expanded its store network and made investments in cutting-edge equipment and goods using business financing.

To fund the development of new stores and implement innovations like mobile ordering and payment methods, Starbucks acquired loans and lines of credit. Its continued growth was aided by this credit assistance.

- **Tesla**

To develop and mass-produce electric vehicles, Tesla, the electric vehicle manufacturer, combined business credit, investment, and strategic alliances. To finance its R&D and production activities, Tesla issued corporate bonds along with loans and credit lines. Tesla became a market leader in the electric car sector because of these financial tactics.

These case studies demonstrate how companies may successfully use several types of corporate credit, such as loans, lines of credit, and financial alliances, to foster development, innovation, and market supremacy. For long-term success, it's crucial to handle corporate credit effectively and properly, since improper or excessive credit management may cause financial difficulties.

Conclusion

The mastery of this financial instrument holds the key to releasing your company's full potential for development and wealth, it is abundantly obvious as we come to the end of our adventure through the world of business credit. We have looked at the key ideas, tactics, and perceptions required to harness the revolutionary potential of business finance throughout this book. You now have access to a wide range of tools that can help you achieve financial success, from establishing SMART objectives to navigating the credit environment and managing credit well.

Business credit is a strategic asset that may help your company reach new heights and is not merely a financial statistic. It serves as a conduit between your goals and their accomplishment, the force behind your growth, and the basis of your commercial partnerships.

You have gained the following knowledge in your quest to master business credit:

- Define Your Vision: Your financial objectives are guided by your vision. It's the energy that propels your company ahead and gives your financial goals purpose.

- Balance your short- and long-term objectives. You've learned the value of establishing goals that include both short-term demands and long-term ambitions since doing so will help you move swiftly through the changing environment of entrepreneurship.

- Establish SMART Objectives: Now that you know how important it is to develop specific, measurable, attainable, relevant, and time-bound goals, you can make sure that your goals are measurable, actionable, and observable.

- Align the Business and Financial Objectives: You've built a solid foundation for long-term success by coordinating your financial objectives with your overall company strategy. This also ensures that every financial choice you make serves to further your purpose.

- Utilise Commercial Credit: You've come to see business credit as a dynamic instrument that helps you access money, improves your credit standing, lowers your risk, and supports the growth of your company.

- Create a Solid Credit Foundation: You now grasp the essential procedures needed to develop a solid credit foundation, from comprehending business credit to creating your company's credit profile to maintaining a spotless personal credit history.

It's crucial to stress in this last chapter that learning how to manage corporate credit is a lifelong process. The concepts and tactics presented in this book are flexible and may be tailored to your changing requirements and objectives for your organization. Keep in mind that perseverance, knowledge, and flexibility are your friends as you pursue your goal of realizing your financial potential.

The financial success of your company is a result of your hard effort as well as your commitment to sound financial judgment and knowledge. Make use of the resources you have learned and the skills you have acquired to guide your company toward a prosperous, successful future.

Keep in mind that your dedication to the financial health of your company will be shown by the route you take as you negotiate the challenging landscape of business credit. You are well-equipped to handle business credit and convert your goals into a flourishing reality with the appropriate mentality and tactical approach.

We appreciate you joining us on this adventure and wish you success and happiness on your way to financial wealth.

Securing Financial Prosperity by Mastering Business Credit

You have started a transforming journey in your quest for financial security; this trip has given you the information and resources you need to master the art of business credit. You've discovered the keys to realizing this priceless financial tool's full potential and realized that it's more than just a measure; it's a strategic asset that can take your company to new heights.

You've learned how to visualize the future you want for your business by defining SMART goals—specific, measurable, attainable, relevant, and time-bound—that will direct your steps. Recognizing that achieving financial success is a crucial component of your larger objective, you have synchronized your company and financial goals.

Your command of business credit has given you access to a vast array of possibilities. It has evolved into your go-to growth partner, a support system through trying times, and a reliable brand that draws both partners and clients. Your goals and realities may be bridged with the help of business credit, which also serves as the foundation for your financial stability.

But keep in mind that this is just the start of the journey—it doesn't mark the conclusion. Here are some last words of advice as you go forward:

- Develop financial literacy: Maintain your education and broaden your financial understanding. One aspect of the complicated financial landscape is business credit. You can make better selections the more you comprehend.
- Be Flexible: The commercial environment is rapidly changing. Be willing to adapt your tactics and objectives as needed. A key quality for achieving financial success is flexibility.
- Network and Collaborate: Establish trusting bonds with colleagues, mentors, and advisers who can provide support, advice, and assistance while you negotiate the complex financial aspects of your company.
- Monitor and Reflect: Keep an eye on your development while periodically analyzing your financial objectives and credit

history. Make judgments based on this knowledge.

- Give Back: As you become financially successful, think about how you may utilize your wealth to benefit your town, industry, or the whole planet.

Now that you have the information, abilities, and insight needed, you can manage company credit and find the financial success you want. May your trip be one of progress, security, and the accomplishment of your most ardent aspirations as you proceed.

Keep in mind that the trip to financial wealth is a shared one; it is not a solo one. Your business and the lives of individuals you come in contact with are both impacted by the success you achieve. May your knowledge of business credit not only improve your life but serve as an example to others who want to reach their financial goals.

The future is yours to create with effort, tenacity, and a smart approach to business finance. Prosper as you go. Your earning potential is limitless, and the world is eagerly awaiting the contribution you are meant to make.